This Book Belongs to:

Soggy Nomad Press
Las Vegas, Nevada, USA

ISBN: 978-1-957532-46-2

www.SoggyNomadPress.com

Cover design by Nola Lee Kelsey

2025

January

S	M	T	W	T	F	S
			1	2	3	4
5	6	7	8	9	10	11
12	13	14	15	16	17	18
19	20	21	22	23	24	25
26	27	28	29	30	31	

February

S	M	T	W	T	F	S
						1
2	3	4	5	6	7	8
9	10	11	12	13	14	15
16	17	18	19	20	21	22
23	24	25	26	27	28	

March

S	M	T	W	T	F	S
						1
2	3	4	5	6	7	8
9	10	11	12	13	14	15
16	17	18	19	20	21	22
23	24	25	26	27	28	29
30	31					

April

S	M	T	W	T	F	S
		1	2	3	4	5
6	7	8	9	10	11	12
13	14	15	16	17	18	19
20	21	22	23	24	25	26
27	28	29	30			

May

S	M	T	W	T	F	S
				1	2	3
4	5	6	7	8	9	10
11	12	13	14	15	16	17
18	19	20	21	22	23	24
25	26	27	28	29	30	31

June

S	M	T	W	T	F	S
1	2	3	4	5	6	7
8	9	10	11	12	13	14
15	16	17	18	19	20	21
22	23	24	25	26	27	28
29	30					

July

S	M	T	W	T	F	S
		1	2	3	4	5
6	7	8	9	10	11	12
13	14	15	16	17	18	19
20	21	22	23	24	25	26
27	28	29	30	31		

August

S	M	T	W	T	F	S
					1	2
3	4	5	6	7	8	9
10	11	12	13	14	15	16
17	18	19	20	21	22	23
24	25	26	27	28	29	30
31						

September

S	M	T	W	T	F	S
	1	2	3	4	5	6
7	8	9	10	11	12	13
14	15	16	17	18	19	20
21	22	23	24	25	26	27
28	29	30				

October

S	M	T	W	T	F	S
			1	2	3	4
5	6	7	8	9	10	11
12	13	14	15	16	17	18
19	20	21	22	23	24	25
26	27	28	29	30	31	

November

S	M	T	W	T	F	S
						1
2	3	4	5	6	7	8
9	10	11	12	13	14	15
16	17	18	19	20	21	22
23	24	25	26	27	28	29
30						

December

S	M	T	W	T	F	S
	1	2	3	4	5	6
7	8	9	10	11	12	13
14	15	16	17	18	19	20
21	22	23	24	25	26	27
28	29	30	31			

Annual Planner

January	February	March

April	May	June

July	August	September

October	November	December

Goals

_____ ☐

_____ ☐

_____ ☐

_____ ☐

_____ ☐

2025

WEEKLY PLANNER

December

○ 30. MONDAY

Shopping

_____

_____

○ 31. TUESDAY

_____

_____

_____

_____

○ 1. WEDNESDAY

TO DO

_____

○ 2. THURSDAY

_____

_____

_____

_____

○ 3. FRIDAY

_____

_____

_____

○ 4. SATURDAY / 5. SUNDAY

_____

_____

_____

January

01/06/25 - 01/12/25

◯ 6. MONDAY

Shopping

_____

_____

◯ 7. TUESDAY

_____

_____

_____

_____

_____

◯ 8. WEDNESDAY

TO DO

_____

_____

◯ 9. THURSDAY

_____

_____

_____

_____

_____

◯ 10. FRIDAY

_____

_____

_____

_____

◯ 11. SATURDAY / 12. SUNDAY

_____

_____

_____

_____

January

01/13/25 - 01/19/25

○ 13. MONDAY

Shopping

_____

_____

○ 14. TUESDAY

_____

_____

_____

_____

○ 15. WEDNESDAY

_____

TO DO

_____

_____

○ 16. THURSDAY

_____

_____

_____

_____

○ 17. FRIDAY

_____

_____

_____

_____

○ 18. SATURDAY / 19. SUNDAY

_____

_____

_____

_____

January

01/20/25 - 01/26/25

○ 20. MONDAY

Shopping

○ 21. TUESDAY

○ 22. WEDNESDAY

TO DO

○ 23. THURSDAY

○ 24. FRIDAY

○ 25. SATURDAY / 26. SUNDAY

January

○ 27. MONDAY

Shopping

_____

_____

○ 28. TUESDAY

_____

_____

_____

_____

○ 29. WEDNESDAY

TO DO

_____

○ 30. THURSDAY

_____

_____

_____

○ 31. FRIDAY

_____

_____

_____

○ 1. SATURDAY / 2. SUNDAY

_____

_____

February

○ 3. MONDAY

Shopping

○ 4. TUESDAY

○ 5. WEDNESDAY

TO DO

○ 6. THURSDAY

○ 7. FRIDAY

○ 8. SATURDAY / 9. SUNDAY

Yorkie Love!

Valentine's Day

February

Week 7

○ 10. MONDAY

Shopping

_____

_____

○ 11. TUESDAY

_____

_____

_____

_____

○ 12. WEDNESDAY

TO DO

_____

_____

○ 13. THURSDAY

_____

_____

_____

_____

○ 14. FRIDAY

_____

_____

_____

_____

○ 15. SATURDAY / 16. SUNDAY

_____

_____

_____

February

02/17/25 - 02/23/25

○ 17. MONDAY

Shopping

○ 18. TUESDAY

○ 19. WEDNESDAY

TO DO

○ 20. THURSDAY

○ 21. FRIDAY

○ 22. SATURDAY / 23. SUNDAY

February

○ 24. MONDAY

Shopping

○ 25. TUESDAY

○ 26. WEDNESDAY

TO DO

○ 27. THURSDAY

○ 28. FRIDAY

○ 1. SATURDAY / 2. SUNDAY

March

03/03/25 - 03/09/25

○ 3. MONDAY

Shopping

○ 4. TUESDAY

○ 5. WEDNESDAY

TO DO

○ 6. THURSDAY

○ 7. FRIDAY

○ 8. SATURDAY / 9. SUNDAY

March

Week 11

03/10/25 - 03/16/25

○ 10. MONDAY

Shopping

_____

_____

○ 11. TUESDAY

_____

_____

_____

_____

○ 12. WEDNESDAY

TO DO

_____

_____

○ 13. THURSDAY

_____

_____

_____

○ 14. FRIDAY

_____

_____

_____

_____

○ 15. SATURDAY / 16. SUNDAY

_____

_____

_____

Yorkie

Saint Patrick's Day

March

03/17/25 - 03/23/25

○ 17. MONDAY

Shopping

_____

_____

○ 18. TUESDAY

_____

_____

_____

_____

_____

○ 19. WEDNESDAY

TO DO

_____

_____

○ 20. THURSDAY

_____

_____

_____

_____

○ 21. FRIDAY

_____

_____

_____

_____

○ 22. SATURDAY / 23. SUNDAY

_____

_____

_____

_____

March

03/24/25 - 03/30/25

○ 24. MONDAY

Shopping

_____

_____

○ 25. TUESDAY

_____

_____

_____

_____

○ 26. WEDNESDAY

TO DO

_____

○ 27. THURSDAY

_____

_____

_____

○ 28. FRIDAY

_____

_____

_____

○ 29. SATURDAY / 30. SUNDAY

_____

_____

_____

March

○ 31. MONDAY

Shopping
_____
_____
_____
_____
_____
_____

○ 1. TUESDAY

○ 2. WEDNESDAY

TO DO
_____
_____
_____
_____

○ 3. THURSDAY

_____
_____
_____

○ 4. FRIDAY

_____
_____
_____
_____

○ 5. SATURDAY / 6. SUNDAY

_____
_____
_____
_____

April

Week 15

04/07/25 - 04/13/25

○ 7. MONDAY

Shopping

○ 8. TUESDAY

○ 9. WEDNESDAY

TO DO

○ 10. THURSDAY

○ 11. FRIDAY

○ 12. SATURDAY / 13. SUNDAY

The Easter

Yorkie

April

Week 16

04/14/25 - 04/20/25

○ 14. MONDAY

Shopping
_____
_____
○ 15. TUESDAY
_____
_____
_____
_____

○ 16. WEDNESDAY

TO DO
_____
_____
○ 17. THURSDAY
_____
_____
_____
_____
○ 18. FRIDAY
_____
_____
_____
○ 19. SATURDAY / 20. SUNDAY
_____
_____
_____

April

04/21/25 - 04/27/25

○ 21. MONDAY

Shopping

○ 22. TUESDAY

○ 23. WEDNESDAY

TO DO

○ 24. THURSDAY

○ 25. FRIDAY

○ 26. SATURDAY / 27. SUNDAY

April

Week 18

04/28/25 - 05/04/25

○ 28. MONDAY

Shopping

○ 29. TUESDAY

○ 30. WEDNESDAY

TO DO

○ 1. THURSDAY

○ 2. FRIDAY

○ 3. SATURDAY / 4. SUNDAY

May

Week 19

05/05/25 - 05/11/25

○ 5. MONDAY

Shopping

_____

_____

○ 6. TUESDAY

_____

_____

_____

_____

○ 7. WEDNESDAY

TO DO

_____

_____

○ 8. THURSDAY

_____

_____

_____

_____

○ 9. FRIDAY

_____

_____

_____

_____

○ 10. SATURDAY / 11. SUNDAY

_____

_____

_____

_____

May

Week 20

○ 12. MONDAY

Shopping

_____

_____

○ 13. TUESDAY

_____

_____

_____

_____

○ 14. WEDNESDAY

TO DO

_____

○ 15. THURSDAY

_____

_____

_____

○ 16. FRIDAY

_____

_____

_____

○ 17. SATURDAY / 18. SUNDAY

_____

_____

_____

_____

May

○ 19. MONDAY

Shopping

○ 20. TUESDAY

○ 21. WEDNESDAY

TO DO

○ 22. THURSDAY

○ 23. FRIDAY

○ 24. SATURDAY / 25. SUNDAY

May

Week 22

05/26/25 - 06/01/25

○ 26. MONDAY

Shopping

○ 27. TUESDAY

○ 28. WEDNESDAY

TO DO

○ 29. THURSDAY

○ 30. FRIDAY

○ 31. SATURDAY / 1. SUNDAY

June

06/02/25 - 06/08/25

○ 2. MONDAY

Shopping

_____

_____

○ 3. TUESDAY

_____

_____

_____

_____

○ 4. WEDNESDAY

_____

TO DO

_____

_____

○ 5. THURSDAY

_____

_____

_____

_____

○ 6. FRIDAY

_____

_____

_____

_____

○ 7. SATURDAY / 8. SUNDAY

_____

_____

_____

_____

June

Week 24

06/09/25 - 06/15/25

○ 9. MONDAY

Shopping

○ 10. TUESDAY

○ 11. WEDNESDAY

TO DO

○ 12. THURSDAY

○ 13. FRIDAY

○ 14. SATURDAY / 15. SUNDAY

June

○ 16. MONDAY

Shopping

_____

_____

_____

○ 17. TUESDAY

_____

_____

_____

○ 18. WEDNESDAY

TO DO

_____

○ 19. THURSDAY

_____

_____

_____

_____

○ 20. FRIDAY

_____

_____

_____

○ 21. SATURDAY / 22. SUNDAY

_____

_____

_____

June

Week 26   06/23/25 - 06/29/25

○ 23. MONDAY

Shopping

○ 24. TUESDAY

○ 25. WEDNESDAY

TO DO

○ 26. THURSDAY

○ 27. FRIDAY

○ 28. SATURDAY / 29. SUNDAY

HAPPY

YORK OF JULY

June

○ 30. MONDAY

Shopping

_____

_____

○ 1. TUESDAY

_____

_____

_____

_____

○ 2. WEDNESDAY

TO DO

_____

_____

○ 3. THURSDAY

_____

_____

_____

_____

○ 4. FRIDAY

_____

_____

_____

_____

○ 5. SATURDAY / 6. SUNDAY

_____

_____

_____

July

07/07/25 - 07/13/25

○ 7. MONDAY

Shopping

○ 8. TUESDAY

○ 9. WEDNESDAY

TO DO

○ 10. THURSDAY

○ 11. FRIDAY

○ 12. SATURDAY / 13. SUNDAY

July

Week 29

07/14/25 - 07/20/25

○ 14. MONDAY

Shopping

○ 15. TUESDAY

○ 16. WEDNESDAY

TO DO

○ 17. THURSDAY

○ 18. FRIDAY

○ 19. SATURDAY / 20. SUNDAY

July

Week 30

07/21/25 - 07/27/25

○ 21. MONDAY

Shopping

○ 22. TUESDAY

○ 23. WEDNESDAY

TO DO

○ 24. THURSDAY

○ 25. FRIDAY

○ 26. SATURDAY / 27. SUNDAY

July

07/28/25 - 08/03/25

○ 28. MONDAY

Shopping

_____

_____

_____

○ 29. TUESDAY

_____

_____

_____

_____

○ 30. WEDNESDAY

TO DO

_____

_____

○ 31. THURSDAY

_____

_____

_____

_____

○ 1. FRIDAY

_____

_____

_____

_____

○ 2. SATURDAY / 3. SUNDAY

_____

_____

_____

_____

August

Week 32

08/04/25 - 08/10/25

○ 4. MONDAY

Shopping

_____

_____

○ 5. TUESDAY

_____

_____

_____

_____

○ 6. WEDNESDAY

TO DO

_____

○ 7. THURSDAY

_____

_____

_____

_____

○ 8. FRIDAY

_____

_____

_____

_____

○ 9. SATURDAY / 10. SUNDAY

_____

_____

_____

August

08/11/25 - 08/17/25

○ 11. MONDAY

Shopping

_____

_____

○ 12. TUESDAY

_____

_____

_____

○ 13. WEDNESDAY

TO DO

_____

_____

○ 14. THURSDAY

_____

_____

_____

_____

○ 15. FRIDAY

_____

_____

_____

_____

○ 16. SATURDAY / 17. SUNDAY

_____

_____

_____

August

08/18/25 - 08/24/25

○ 18. MONDAY

Shopping

_____

_____

○ 19. TUESDAY

_____

_____

_____

_____

○ 20. WEDNESDAY

TO DO

_____

_____

○ 21. THURSDAY

_____

_____

_____

_____

○ 22. FRIDAY

_____

_____

_____

_____

○ 23. SATURDAY / 24. SUNDAY

_____

_____

_____

_____

August

08/25/25 - 08/31/25

○ 25. MONDAY

Shopping

_____
_____
○ 26. TUESDAY   _____
_____
_____
_____
_____
○ 27. WEDNESDAY

TO DO

_____
_____
○ 28. THURSDAY   _____
_____
_____
_____
_____
_____
○ 29. FRIDAY   _____
_____
_____
_____
_____
○ 30. SATURDAY / 31. SUNDAY   _____
_____
_____
_____

September

09/01/25 - 09/07/25

○ 1. MONDAY

Shopping

○ 2. TUESDAY

○ 3. WEDNESDAY

TO DO

○ 4. THURSDAY

○ 5. FRIDAY

○ 6. SATURDAY / 7. SUNDAY

September

09/08/25 - 09/14/25

○ 8. MONDAY

Shopping

○ 9. TUESDAY

○ 10. WEDNESDAY

TO DO

○ 11. THURSDAY

○ 12. FRIDAY

○ 13. SATURDAY / 14. SUNDAY

September

Week 38

○ 15. MONDAY

Shopping

_____
_____
_____
_____
_____
_____

○ 16. TUESDAY

○ 17. WEDNESDAY

TO DO

_____
_____
_____

○ 18. THURSDAY

_____
_____
_____

○ 19. FRIDAY

_____
_____
_____
_____

○ 20. SATURDAY / 21. SUNDAY

_____
_____
_____

September

09/22/25 - 09/28/25

○ 22. MONDAY

Shopping

○ 23. TUESDAY

○ 24. WEDNESDAY

TO DO

○ 25. THURSDAY

○ 26. FRIDAY

○ 27. SATURDAY / 28. SUNDAY

September

09/29/25 - 10/05/25

○ 29. MONDAY

Shopping

○ 30. TUESDAY

○ 1. WEDNESDAY

TO DO

○ 2. THURSDAY

○ 3. FRIDAY

○ 4. SATURDAY / 5. SUNDAY

October

10/06/25 - 10/12/25

○ 6. MONDAY

Shopping

_____

_____

○ 7. TUESDAY

_____

_____

_____

_____

○ 8. WEDNESDAY

_____

TO DO

_____

_____

○ 9. THURSDAY

_____

_____

_____

_____

○ 10. FRIDAY

_____

_____

_____

_____

○ 11. SATURDAY / 12. SUNDAY

_____

_____

_____

October

10/13/25 - 10/19/25

○ 13. MONDAY

Shopping

_____

_____

○ 14. TUESDAY

_____

_____

_____

_____

○ 15. WEDNESDAY

TO DO

_____

_____

○ 16. THURSDAY

_____

_____

_____

_____

○ 17. FRIDAY

_____

_____

_____

_____

○ 18. SATURDAY / 19. SUNDAY

_____

_____

_____

_____

October

○ 20. MONDAY

Shopping

○ 21. TUESDAY

○ 22. WEDNESDAY

TO DO

○ 23. THURSDAY

○ 24. FRIDAY

○ 25. SATURDAY / 26. SUNDAY

October

Week 44   10/27/25 - 11/02/25

○ 27. MONDAY

Shopping

○ 28. TUESDAY

○ 29. WEDNESDAY

TO DO

○ 30. THURSDAY

○ 31. FRIDAY

○ 1. SATURDAY / 2. SUNDAY

November

Week 45   11/03/25 - 11/09/25

○ 3. MONDAY

Shopping

_____

_____

_____

○ 4. TUESDAY

_____

_____

_____

_____

○ 5. WEDNESDAY

TO DO

_____

_____

○ 6. THURSDAY

_____

_____

_____

_____

○ 7. FRIDAY

_____

_____

_____

_____

○ 8. SATURDAY / 9. SUNDAY

_____

_____

_____

_____

November

11/10/25 - 11/16/25

○ 10. MONDAY

Shopping

_____

_____

○ 11. TUESDAY

_____

_____

_____

_____

○ 12. WEDNESDAY

TO DO

_____

_____

○ 13. THURSDAY

_____

_____

_____

_____

○ 14. FRIDAY

_____

_____

_____

○ 15. SATURDAY / 16. SUNDAY

_____

_____

_____

November

○ 17. MONDAY

Shopping

○ 18. TUESDAY

○ 19. WEDNESDAY

TO DO

○ 20. THURSDAY

○ 21. FRIDAY

○ 22. SATURDAY / 23. SUNDAY

November

11/24/25 - 11/30/25

○ 24. MONDAY

○ 25. TUESDAY

Shopping

_____

_____

_____

_____

_____

_____

○ 26. WEDNESDAY

○ 27. THURSDAY

TO DO

_____

_____

_____

_____

_____

○ 28. FRIDAY

_____

_____

○ 29. SATURDAY / 30. SUNDAY

_____

_____

_____

_____

December

○ 1. MONDAY

Shopping

○ 2. TUESDAY

○ 3. WEDNESDAY

TO DO

○ 4. THURSDAY

○ 5. FRIDAY

○ 6. SATURDAY / 7. SUNDAY

December

12/08/25 - 12/14/25

○ 8. MONDAY

Shopping

_____

_____

○ 9. TUESDAY

_____

_____

_____

○ 10. WEDNESDAY

_____

TO DO

_____

○ 11. THURSDAY

_____

_____

_____

_____

○ 12. FRIDAY

_____

_____

_____

○ 13. SATURDAY / 14. SUNDAY

_____

_____

_____

_____

December

○ 15. MONDAY

Shopping

_____

_____

○ 16. TUESDAY

_____

_____

_____

_____

○ 17. WEDNESDAY

_____

TO DO

_____

○ 18. THURSDAY

_____

_____

_____

_____

○ 19. FRIDAY

_____

_____

_____

_____

○ 20. SATURDAY / 21. SUNDAY

_____

_____

_____

_____

Merry

Yorkie
Christmas

December

12/22/25 - 12/28/25

○ 22. MONDAY

Shopping

_____

○ 23. TUESDAY

_____

_____

_____

_____

○ 24. WEDNESDAY

TO DO

_____

_____

○ 25. THURSDAY

_____

_____

_____

○ 26. FRIDAY

_____

_____

_____

○ 27. SATURDAY / 28. SUNDAY

_____

_____

_____

December

12/29/25 - 01/04/26

○ 29. MONDAY

Shopping

○ 30. TUESDAY

○ 31. WEDNESDAY

TO DO

○ 1. THURSDAY

○ 2. FRIDAY

○ 3. SATURDAY / 4. SUNDAY

January 2025

Sun	Mon	Tue	Wed	Thu	Fri	Sat
29	30	31	1	2	3	4
5	6	7	8	9	10	11
12	13	14	15	16	17	18
19	20	21	22	23	24	25
26	27	28	29	30	31	1

February 2025

Sun	Mon	Tue	Wed	Thu	Fri	Sat
26	27	28	29	30	31	1
2	3	4	5	6	7	8
9	10	11	12	13	14	15
16	17	18	19	20	21	22
23	24	25	26	27	28	1

_____

_____

_____

_____

March 2025

Sun	Mon	Tue	Wed	Thu	Fri	Sat
23	24	25	26	27	28	1
2	3	4	5	6	7	8
9	10	11	12	13	14	15
16	17	18	19	20	21	22
23	24	25	26	27	28	29
30	31	1	2	3	4	5

April 2025

Sun	Mon	Tue	Wed	Thu	Fri	Sat
30	31	1	2	3	4	5
6	7	8	9	10	11	12
13	14	15	16	17	18	19
20	21	22	23	24	25	26
27	28	29	30	1	2	3

_____

_____

_____

_____

May 2025

Sun	Mon	Tue	Wed	Thu	Fri	Sat
27	28	29	30	1	2	3
4	5	6	7	8	9	10
11	12	13	14	15	16	17
18	19	20	21	22	23	24
25	26	27	28	29	30	31

June 2025

Sun	Mon	Tue	Wed	Thu	Fri	Sat
1	2	3	4	5	6	7
8	9	10	11	12	13	14
15	16	17	18	19	20	21
22	23	24	25	26	27	28
29	30	1	2	3	4	5

_____

_____

_____

_____

July 2025

Sun	Mon	Tue	Wed	Thu	Fri	Sat
29	30	1	2	3	4	5
6	7	8	9	10	11	12
13	14	15	16	17	18	19
20	21	22	23	24	25	26
27	28	29	30	31	1	2

_____
_____
_____
_____

August 2025

Sun	Mon	Tue	Wed	Thu	Fri	Sat
27	28	29	30	31	1	2
3	4	5	6	7	8	9
10	11	12	13	14	15	16
17	18	19	20	21	22	23
24	25	26	27	28	29	30
31	1	2	3	4	5	6

_____

_____

_____

_____

September 2025

Sun	Mon	Tue	Wed	Thu	Fri	Sat
31	1	2	3	4	5	6
7	8	9	10	11	12	13
14	15	16	17	18	19	20
21	22	23	24	25	26	27
28	29	30	1	2	3	4

October 2025

Sun	Mon	Tue	Wed	Thu	Fri	Sat
28	29	30	1	2	3	4
5	6	7	8	9	10	11
12	13	14	15	16	17	18
19	20	21	22	23	24	25
26	27	28	29	30	31	1

_____

_____

_____

_____

November 2025

Sun	Mon	Tue	Wed	Thu	Fri	Sat
26	27	28	29	30	31	1
2	3	4	5	6	7	8
9	10	11	12	13	14	15
16	17	18	19	20	21	22
23	24	25	26	27	28	29
30	1	2	3	4	5	6

_____

_____

_____

_____

December 2025

Sun	Mon	Tue	Wed	Thu	Fri	Sat
30	1	2	3	4	5	6
7	8	9	10	11	12	13
14	15	16	17	18	19	20
21	22	23	24	25	26	27
28	29	30	31	1	2	3

_____

_____

_____

_____

Contacts

Name

Address

City   State   Zip

Phone

Email

Name

Address

City   State   Zip

Phone

Email

Name

Address

City   State   Zip

Phone

Email

Name

Address

City   State   Zip

Phone

Email

Name

Address

City   State   Zip

Phone

Email

Name

Address

City   State   Zip

Phone

Email

Name

Address

City   State   Zip

Phone

Email

Name

Address

City   State   Zip

Phone

Email

Name

Address

City   State   Zip

Phone

Email

Name

Address

City   State   Zip

Phone

Email

Contacts

Name

Address

City   State   Zip

Phone

Email

Name

Address

City   State   Zip

Phone

Email

Name

Address

City   State   Zip

Phone

Email

Name

Address

City   State   Zip

Phone

Email

Name

Address

City   State   Zip

Phone

Email

Name

Address

City   State   Zip

Phone

Email

Name

Address

City   State   Zip

Phone

Email

Name

Address

City   State   Zip

Phone

Email

Name

Address

City   State   Zip

Phone

Email

Name

Address

City   State   Zip

Phone

Email

Contacts

Name

Address

City   State   Zip

Phone

Email

Name

Address

City   State   Zip

Phone

Email

Name

Address

City   State   Zip

Phone

Email

Name

Address

City   State   Zip

Phone

Email

Name

Address

City   State   Zip

Phone

Email

Name

Address

City   State   Zip

Phone

Email

Name

Address

City   State   Zip

Phone

Email

Name

Address

City   State   Zip

Phone

Email

Name

Address

City   State   Zip

Phone

Email

Name

Address

City   State   Zip

Phone

Email

Passwords

Website	
Username	
Password	
Email	
Notes	

Website	
Username	
Password	
Email	
Notes	

Website	
Username	
Password	
Email	
Notes	

Website	
Username	
Password	
Email	
Notes	

Website	
Username	
Password	
Email	
Notes	

Website	
Username	
Password	
Email	
Notes	

Website	
Username	
Password	
Email	
Notes	

Website	
Username	
Password	
Email	
Notes	

Passwords

Website	
Username	
Password	
Email	
Notes	

Website	
Username	
Password	
Email	
Notes	

Website	
Username	
Password	
Email	
Notes	

Website	
Username	
Password	
Email	
Notes	

Website	
Username	
Password	
Email	
Notes	

Website	
Username	
Password	
Email	
Notes	

Website	
Username	
Password	
Email	
Notes	

Website	
Username	
Password	
Email	
Notes	

Passwords

Website	
Username	
Password	
Email	
Notes	

Website	
Username	
Password	
Email	
Notes	

Website	
Username	
Password	
Email	
Notes	

Website	
Username	
Password	
Email	
Notes	

Website	
Username	
Password	
Email	
Notes	

Website	
Username	
Password	
Email	
Notes	

Website	
Username	
Password	
Email	
Notes	

Website	
Username	
Password	
Email	
Notes	

Notes

Notes

Notes

Notes

2026

January

S	M	T	W	T	F	S
				1	2	3
4	5	6	7	8	9	10
11	12	13	14	15	16	17
18	19	20	21	22	23	24
25	26	27	28	29	30	31

February

S	M	T	W	T	F	S
1	2	3	4	5	6	7
8	9	10	11	12	13	14
15	16	17	18	19	20	21
22	23	24	25	26	27	28

March

S	M	T	W	T	F	S
1	2	3	4	5	6	7
8	9	10	11	12	13	14
15	16	17	18	19	20	21
22	23	24	25	26	27	28
29	30	31				

April

S	M	T	W	T	F	S
			1	2	3	4
5	6	7	8	9	10	11
12	13	14	15	16	17	18
19	20	21	22	23	24	25
26	27	28	29	30		

May

S	M	T	W	T	F	S
					1	2
3	4	5	6	7	8	9
10	11	12	13	14	15	16
17	18	19	20	21	22	23
24	25	26	27	28	29	30
31						

June

S	M	T	W	T	F	S
	1	2	3	4	5	6
7	8	9	10	11	12	13
14	15	16	17	18	19	20
21	22	23	24	25	26	27
28	29	30				

July

S	M	T	W	T	F	S
			1	2	3	4
5	6	7	8	9	10	11
12	13	14	15	16	17	18
19	20	21	22	23	24	25
26	27	28	29	30	31	

August

S	M	T	W	T	F	S
						1
2	3	4	5	6	7	8
9	10	11	12	13	14	15
16	17	18	19	20	21	22
23	24	25	26	27	28	29
30	31					

September

S	M	T	W	T	F	S
		1	2	3	4	5
6	7	8	9	10	11	12
13	14	15	16	17	18	19
20	21	22	23	24	25	26
27	28	29	30			

October

S	M	T	W	T	F	S
				1	2	3
4	5	6	7	8	9	10
11	12	13	14	15	16	17
18	19	20	21	22	23	24
25	26	27	28	29	30	31

November

S	M	T	W	T	F	S
1	2	3	4	5	6	7
8	9	10	11	12	13	14
15	16	17	18	19	20	21
22	23	24	25	26	27	28
29	30					

December

S	M	T	W	T	F	S
		1	2	3	4	5
6	7	8	9	10	11	12
13	14	15	16	17	18	19
20	21	22	23	24	25	26
27	28	29	30	31		

Pee You

Next Year

From Nola Lee Kelsey & Soggy Nomad Press